D1825092

Poems For Fun

This book is full of all kinds of poems about all kinds of fun – games, riddles, parties, even school – and is both an excellent introduction to the pleasures of reading verse for young people and thoroughly enjoyable as well.

Ian Woodward specialises in writing about the theatre, films and music, and together with his Czech-born wife Zenka was the editor of another Beaver poetry anthology, *The Beaver Book of Creepy Verse*. The Woodwards live in a Hertfordshire village and have two small children.

Poems For Fun

chosen by Zenka and Ian Woodward

Illustrated by Tony Escott

Beaver Books

First published in 1983 by
The Hamlyn Publishing Group Limited
London · New York · Sydney · Toronto
Astronaut House, Feltham, Middlesex, England

© Copyright this collection
Zenka and Ian Woodward 1983
© Copyright Illustrations
The Hamlyn Publishing Group Limited 1983
ISBN 0 600 20610 6

Printed and bound in Great Britain by
Cox & Wyman Limited, Reading
Set in Souvenir

FOR
PHILIP and STEFANIE

Contents

Have a lot of fun!

All the poems in this book have one thing in common: a sense of *fun*. They are designed to cheer you up, make you smile, give you something to think about and even test your skills at working out puzzles and solving riddles. There are some poems whose lines make funny shapes and other poems whose words mischievously run right off the page and into your hand.

Some poems tell of the 'fun things' which all young people enjoy doing – like blowing toy trumpets, banging biscuit tins, making paper boats, trying to knit, flying kites, having delicious tea parties, playing cowboys and Indians and ball games and shuttlecock and marbles and going higher and higher on the garden swing.

'Fun things', too, like skipping, going to camp, leaving school when the four o'clock bell rings, waving to engine drivers as the trains go whistling by, pulling faces at old Uncle Umbert who wears such a frown, asking lots and lots of questions – *'What makes the glow-worm glow?'*, *'Who walks on the bridge of the nose?'*, climbing trees, staying up late, and eating eggs and bacon and chips and ice-cream and jam.

We have also included plenty of fun-poems about numbers and the letters of the alphabet, and game-poems which you and all your family and friends can join in and 'act out' and make lots of wonderful sound-effects. There are tongue-twisters – *'I wish I was washed like car-washes wash cars'* – picture-puzzle poems, and even poems about tumbling into bed at night.

People who write poems are often accused of

not having fun any more. They are said to be far too serious. Well, we are glad to say that this is not true of the writers whose poems appear in this book.

Start at the beginning of the book and work through to the end. Or just open the book wherever you fancy. But whatever you do, we can promise you one thing: you will have a lot of

FUN!

Zenka Woodward

Ian Woodward

Editors' note

You have probably noticed that in some books of verse there are many poems written by 'Anon' and 'Unknown'. But who are, or rather *were*, they? Well, they were poets who were so mysterious that today we do not know their names. They are simply *unknown* – or *anonymous*, which means the same thing. So where a name does not appear at the end of a poem in this book, you can be sure that the poet's identity is still a mystery.

1
A Fun-packed Day

Morning prayer

Now another day is breaking,
Sleep was sweet and so is waking.
Dear Lord, I promised you last night
Never again to sulk or fight.
Such vows are easier to keep
When a child is sound asleep.
Today, O Lord, for your dear sake,
I'll try to keep them when awake.

Ogden Nash

The milkman

Clink, clink, clinkety clink.
The milkman's on his rounds, I think.
Crunch, crunch come the milkman's feet
Closer and closer along the street—
Then clink, clink, clinkety-clink,
He's left our bottles of milk to drink.

Clive Sansom

Ruth is six

A mobile floats above her bed
Of fishes, green and grey,
That move on drifting waves of air
As night gives place to day.

And Ruth, her eyes still dimmed with sleep,
Lies blissfully aware
Of her lazy mermaid's waving tail,
And seaweed through her hair.

Lydia Pender

Thinking in bed

I won a battle yesterday;
I might win again today—
That is if I decide to play
With my fort.
I might decide to play in my hideaway
And be Robinson Crusoe, or a cave man,
Or just a wild animal in his den.
But there again,
I might decide to play with
The boy next door, cops and robbers:
But I'd have to win, just to even up the score.
(What if he's out?) And as I think some more
Mother opens the bedroom door:
'Come on, Jimmy, it's school today—
No time for day-dreaming, no time with your toys
    to play.'
Silly me.
O bother, I thought it was Sunday!

S. L. Dayman

Late for breakfast

Who is it hides my sandals when I'm trying to get
    dressed?
And takes away the hairbrush that was lying on
    the chest?
I wanted to start breakfast before any of the
    others
But something's always missing or been
    borrowed by my brothers.
I think I'd better dress at night, and eat my
    breakfast too,
      Then when everybody's hurrying—
      I'll have nothing else to do.

Mary Dawson

Come with me

Come with me, just come with me
To the country, to our little farm.
Come with me, come and see
How simple and happy life can be.
Get up at six and see the dawn;
Shake yourself, wake yourself,
Cast off that yawn,
And awake to the beauty of the earth.
Come with me, come with me,
Walk along the hedgerows:
See the birds in flight,
See the creatures of the woods
Working day and night.
Hear their song, their mating calls;
See the creatures big and small
Become a part of it all . . .
Just come along with me.

S. L. Dayman

2
Fun For Kids
Only

When I grow up

When I grow up,
I think I'll be
A detective
With a skeleton key.

I could be a soldier
And a sailor too;
I'd like to be a keeper
At the public zoo.

I'll own a trumpet
And I'll play a tune;
I'll keep a space ship
To explore the moon.

I'll be a cowboy
And live in the saddle;
I'll be a guide
With a canoe and a paddle.

I'd like to be the driver
On a diesel train;
And it must be fun
To run a building crane.

I'll live in a lighthouse
And guard the shore;
And I know I'll want to be
A dozen things more.

For the more a boy lives
The more a boy learns—
I think I'll be all of them
By taking turns.

William Wise

Babytalk

When you're a GROWN-UP
a SERIOUS and SENSIBLE PERSON
When you've stopped being SILLY
you can go out and have babies
and go into a SERIOUS and SENSIBLE shop
and ask for:
Tuftytails, Paddipads, Bikkipegs, Cosytoes
and
Tommy Tippee Teethers.
Sno-bunnies, Visivents, Safeshines
Combybaths, Dikkybibs
and
Babywipes.
Rumba Rattles and Trigger Jiggers
A Whirlee Three, a Finger Flip
or A Quacky Duck.
And if you're very SENSIBLE
you can choose
Easifitz, Babybuggies and a Safesitterstand.
Or is it a
Saferstandsit?
No it's a Sitstandsafe. I can never remember.
I'm sorry but Babytalk is a very difficult
    language.
It's for adults only.
Like 'X' films
Much too horrible for children.

Michael Rosen

Quiet fun

My son Augustus, in the street, one day,
    Was feeling quite exceptionally merry.
A stranger asked him: 'Can you show me, pray,
    The quickest way to Brompton Cemetery?'
'The quickest way? You bet I can!' said Gus,
And pushed the fellow underneath a bus.

Whatever people say about my son,
He does enjoy his little bit of fun.

Harry Graham

Family court

One would be in less danger
From the wiles of the stranger
If one's own kin and kith
Were more fun to be with.

Ogden Nash

Mother, mother

Mother, mother, what is that,
Hanging down that lady's back?
Hush, my child, you naughty thing!
That's the lady's corset string!

Amelia

Amelia mixed the mustard,
   She mixed it good and thick;
She put it in the custard
   And made her Mother sick,
And showing satisfaction
   By many a loud hurrah,
'Observe,' she said, 'the action
   Of mustard on Mamma.'

A. E. Housman

Toothpaste

Who's been at the toothpaste?
I know some of you do it right
and you squeeze the tube from the bottom
and you roll up the tube as it gets used up,
    don't you?

But somebody
somebody here—
you know who you are
you dig your thumb in
anywhere, anyhow
and you've turned that tube of toothpaste
into a squashed sock.
You've made it so hard to use
it's like trying to get toothpaste
out of a packet of nuts.

You know who you are.
I won't ask you to come out here now
but you know who you are.

And then you went and left the top off,
    didn't you?
So the toothpaste turned to cement.

People who do things like that should . . .
you should be ashamed of yourself.

I am.

                                        Michael Rosen

18

Birthday

It's my birthday today,
And I'm nine.
I'm having a party tonight,
And we'll play on the lawn
If it's fine.
There'll be John, Dick and Jim,
And Alan and Tim,
And Dennis and Brian and Hugh;
But the star of the show,
You'll be sorry to know,
Will be Sue.
(She's my sister, aged two,
And she'll yell till she's blue
In the face, and be sick.)

Noise

Billy is blowing his trumpet,
Bertie is banging a tin;
Betty is crying for Mummy
And Bob has pricked Ben with a pin.
Baby is crying out loudly;
He's out on the lawn in his pram.
I am the only one silent
And I've eaten all of the jam.

Suspension

Out of the window Richard dangles
His Baby-brother at all angles,
Till Baby slips, and on his head
Descends into a flower bed.
Richard at once reports to Mother
The wretched fate of Baby-brother;
And both run down in loving fear
To see what's left of Baby dear.
Mother not only was much pained
To see how little there remained,
But screamed at Richard 'O you silly,
You've dropped him on my favourite lily!'

Guy Boas

What someone said when he was spanked on the day before his birthday

Some day
I may
Pack my bag and run away.
Some day
I may.
– But not today.

Some night
I might
Slip away in the moonlight.
I might
Some night
– But not tonight.

Some night,
Some day,
I might,
I may
– But right now I think I'll stay.

John Ciardi

Did you?

Having little kids around, they say, is truly bliss;
But did you ever hear of any little kid like this?

He swallows pits,
Has temper fits,
Spills the ink,
And clogs the sink.
And, oh my gosh!
He hates to wash!
He plays with matches,
And grabs and snatches.
He scrawls on walls,
And sprawls and bawls,
And argues and fights,
And kicks and bites. . . .
You say you never heard of
    any kid like that, you do—
Well, I know one who's
    just like that and it's
            Y
              O
                U!

William Cole

When I was your age

When I was your age, child—
When I was eight,
When I was ten,
When I was two
(How old are you?)—
When I was your age, child,
My father would have gone quite *wild*
Had I behaved the way you
Do.
What, food uneaten on my plate
When I was eight?
What, room in such a filthy state
When I was ten?
What, late
For school when I was two?
My father would have shouted, 'When
I was was your age, child, my father would have
    raved
Had I behaved
The way you
Do.'

Michael Frayn

Daddy fell into the pond

Everyone grumbled. The sky was grey.
We had nothing to do and nothing to say.
We were nearing the end of a dismal day.
And there seemed to be nothing beyond,
THEN
DADDY FELL INTO THE POND!

And everyone's face grew merry and bright,
And Timothy danced for sheer delight.
'Give me a camera, quick, oh quick!
He's crawling out of the duckweed!' *Click!*

Then the gardener suddenly slapped his knee,
And doubled up, shaking silently,
And the ducks all quacked as if they were daft
And it sounded as if the old drake laughed.
O, there wasn't a thing that didn't respond
WHEN
DADDY FELL INTO THE POND!

Alfred Noyes

You were the mother last time

'You were the mother last time.
It's my turn today.'
        'It's *my* turn.'
'No, *my* turn.'
        'All right then, I won't play.'
'Oh, go ahead then, *be* the mother.
It's not fair
But I don't care.'

'I was the father last time.
I won't be today.'
        'It's your turn.'
'No, *your* turn.'
        'All right then, I won't play.'
'Oh, never mind, *don't* be the father.
It's not fair
But I don't care.'

'I was the sister last time.
It's your turn today.'
        'It is not.'
'It is so.'
        'All right then, I won't play.'
'Oh, never mind, *don't* be the sister.
It's not fair
But I don't care.'

'I have an idea!
Let's *both* be mothers!
(We'll pretend
About the others.)'

                    Mary Ann Hoberman

3
At School

School bell

Nine-o'Clock Bell!
Nine-o'Clock Bell!
All the small children and big ones as well,
Pulling their stockings up, snatching their hats,
Cheeking and grumbling and giving back-chats,
Laughing and quarrelling, dropping their things,
These at a snail's pace and those upon wings,
Lagging behind a bit, running ahead,
Waiting at corners for lights to turn red,
Some of them scurrying,
Others not worrying,
Carelessly trudging or anxiously hurrying,
All through the streets they are coming pell-mell
At the Nine-o'Clock
Nine-o'Clock
Nine-o'Clock
Bell!

Eleanor Farjeon

Bus to school

Rounding the corner
It comes to a stay.
Quick! Grab a rail!
Now we're off on our way . . .
Oh, but it's Thursday,
The day of fear!
Three hateful lessons!
And school draws near.

Here in the bus though
There's plenty to see:
Boys full of talk about
Last night's TV;
Girls with their violins,
Armfuls of twigs
And flowers for teacher;
Bartlett and Biggs;
Conductor who chats with them,
Jokes about cricket;
Machine that flicks out
A white ribbon of ticket . . .
Yes, but it's Thursday,
The day of fear!—
Six hateful lessons!
And school draws near.

Conductor now waiting,
Firm as a rock,
For Billy whose penny's
Slid down in his sock.
Conductor frowning,
Hand on his handle;
Poor Billy blushes,
Undoes his sandal . . .
'Hold very tight, please,
Any more fares?'
Whistling conductor
Goes clumping upstairs . . .
Boots up above now!
Boys coming down! . . .
Over the hump-bridge
And into the town.

Old Warren sweeping
In his shirt-sleeves!
Sun on his shop-front,
Sun on the leaves . . .
Only, it's Thursday,
The day of fear!
All hateful lessons!
And school draws near.

John Walsh

School dinners

If you stay to school dinners
Better throw them aside;
A lot of kids didn't,
A lot of kids died.

The meat is made of iron,
The spuds are made of steel;
And if that don't get you
The afters will!

Streemin

Im in the botom streme
Which meens Im not brigth
dont like reading
cant hardly write

but all these divishns
arnt reely fair
look at the cemtery
no streemin there

Roger McGough

Ten kinds

Winnie Whiney, all things grieve her;
Fannie Fibber, who'd believe her?
Lotty Loozem, late to school, sir;
Albert Allplay, quite a fool, sir;
Kitty Kissem, loved by many,
George Grump, not loved by any;
Ralph Ruff – beware his fist, sir;
Tillie Tattle, like a blister;
Gus Goodactin, bright and cheery;
Sammy Selfish, sour and dreary.
Do you know them, as I've sung them?
Easy 'tis to choose among them.

Mary Mapes Dodge

Out of school

Four o'clock strikes,
There's a rising hum,
Then the doors fly open,
The children come.

With a wild cat-call
And a hop-scotch hop
And a bouncing ball
And a whirling top,

Grazing of knees,
A hair-pull and a slap,
A hitched-up satchel,
A pulled-down cap,

Bully boys reeling off,
Hurt ones squealing off,
Aviators wheeling off,
Mousy ones stealing off,

Woollen gloves for chilblains,
Cotton rags for snufflers,
Pigtails, coat-tails,
Tails of mufflers,

Machine gun cries,
A kennelful of snarlings,
A hurricane of leaves,
A treeful of starlings,

Thinning away now
By some and some,
Thinning away, away,
All gone home.

Hal Summers

4
Family Fun

Folks

I've heard so much
    about other folks' folks,
How somebody's Uncle
    told such jokes
The cat split laughing
    and had to be stitched,
How somebody's Aunt
    got so bewitched
She fried the kettle
    and washed the water
And spanked a letter
    and posted her daughter.
Other folks' folks get so well known,
And nobody knows about my own.

Ted Hughes

Looking forward

When I am grown to man's estate
I shall be very proud and great,
And tell the other girls and boys
Not to meddle with my toys.

Robert Louis Stevenson

My dad

My little
dad
had
five little piggies:
good 'un,
bad 'un,
gay 'un,
sad 'un,
and one little piggie
who was
mad
      mad
           mad!
Five little piggies
had
my little
dad.

Danish nursery rhyme
(translated by N. M. Bodecker)

Magic word

'More jam,' said Rosie to her Mum.
'I want more jam,' said she.
    But no one heard
    The Magic Word.
Mum took a sip of tea.

'The jam! The jam! The jam!' she cried.
Her voice rang loud and clear.
    'I'd like to spread
    It on my bread.'
But no one seemed to hear.

'*Please* pass the jam,' Rose said at last.
Now *that's* the thing to say.
    When Mother heard
    The Magic Word
She passed it right away.

Martin Gardner

Auntie

Auntie, did you feel no pain
  Falling from that apple-tree?
Will you do it, please, again?
  'Cos my friend here didn't see.

Harry Graham

Uncle Ted

Who's that?
That's your Auntie Mabel
and that's me
under the table.

Who's that?
That's Uncle Billy.
Who's that?
Me being silly.

Who's that
licking a lolly?
I'm not sure
but I think it's Polly.

Who's that
behind the tree?
I don't know,
I can't see.
Could be you.
Could be me.

Who's that?
Baby Joe.
Who's that?
I don't know.

Who's that standing
on his head?
Turn it round.

It's Uncle Ted.

Michael Rosen

Uncle Umbert

Here we see old Uncle Umbert,
Wearing such a forlorn frown.
Turn him upside down and you'll see . . .

Uncle Umbert upside down.
What did you expect?

Shel Silverstein

Grandad

every evening after tea
grandad would take his bucket for a walk

An empty bucket

When i asked him why
he said because it was easier to carry
than a full one

grandad had
an answer
for everything

Roger McGough

5
Questions

Questions

I often wonder why, oh why,
All grown-ups say to me:
'When you are old and six foot high,
What do you want to be?'

I sometimes wonder what they'd say
If I should ask them all
What *they* would like to be, if they
Were six years old and small.

Raymond Wilson

Questions

Can you put the spider's web back in place
    That once has been swept away?
Can you put the apple again on the bough
    Which fell at our feet today?
Can you put the lily-cup back on the stem,
    And cause it to live and grow?
Can you mend the butterfly's broken wing
    That you crushed with a hasty blow?
Can you put the bloom again on the grape,
    And the grape again on the vine?
Can you put the dewdrops back on the flowers,
    And make them sparkle and shine?
Can you put the petals back on the rose?
    If you could, would it smell as sweet?
Can you put the flower again on the husk,
    And show me the ripened wheat?
Can you put the kernel back in the nut,
    Or the broken egg in the shell?
Can you put the honey back in the comb,
    And cover with wax each cell?
Can you put the perfume back in the vase
    When once it has sped away?
Can you put the corn-ear back on the corn,
    Or down on the soft earth, say?
You think my questions are trifling, dear?
    Let me ask another one—
Can a hasty word ever be unsaid,
    Or a deed unkind undone?

Questions

Who rode a rhododendron?
Who knows what a willow will owe?
Does an astronaut swoon
When he lands on the moon?
And what makes the glow-worm glow?

Charles Connell

Questions at night

Why
Is the sky?

What starts the thunder overhead?
Who makes the crashing noise?
Are the angels falling out of bed?
Are they breaking all their toys?

Why does the sun go down so soon?
Why do the night-clouds crawl
Hungrily up to the new-laid moon
And swallow it, shell and all?

If there's a Bear among the stars,
As all the people say,
Won't he jump over those pasture-bars
And drink up the Milky Way?

Does every star that happens to fall
Turn into a firefly?
Can't it ever get back to Heaven at all?
And why
Is the sky?

Louis Untermeyer

Foolish questions

Where can a man buy a cap for his knee?
Or a key for the lock of his hair?
And can his eyes be called at school?
I would think – there are pupils there!
What jewels are found in the crown of his head,
And who walks on the bridge of his nose?
Can he use, in building the roof of his mouth,
The nails on the ends of his toes?
Can the crook of his elbow be sent to jail—
If it can, well, then, what did it do?
And how does he sharpen his shoulder blades?
I'll be hanged if I know – do you?
Can he sit in the shade of the palm of his hand,
And beat time with the drum in his ear?
Can the calf of his leg eat the corn on his toe?—

There's somethin' pretty strange around here!

American folk rhyme
(adapted by William Cole)

40

Why?

Why should the world be usual?
   It surely isn't right!
I don't want to confuse you all,
        BUT
   Why shouldn't day be night?

Why shouldn't snow be hot and black?
   Why shouldn't pigs have wings?
Why shouldn't the front be at the back?
        AND
   Why shouldn't dustmen be kings?

Why shouldn't marmalade taste like meat?
   Why shouldn't grass be red?
Why must we always stand on our feet
        WHEN
   We can stand on our head?

Why shouldn't star-fish sing like thrushes?
   Why shouldn't elephants fly?
Why shouldn't pork-pies grow on bushes?
        AND
   Why shouldn't the sea be dry?

I *won't* let the world be usual!
   And if you disagree
I really shall confuse you all,
        'COS
   Why shouldn't you be me?

Raymond Wilson

Why?

Mamma, why is it that the sun
   Shines only in the day?
Why does he shine so nice and warm
   When he's so far away?
Why are the stars so very large?
   Each one looks like a spark.
Why does the moon shine when it's light,
   And never when it's dark?
Why are the summers always warm?
   The winters always cold?
Why is it that each year must die
   When only one year old?
And why can't little children be
   As big as their papas?
And when I ask you questions, Ma,
   Why do you say, 'BECAUSE'?
Why is it, Mamma, when it rains,
   So cloudy in the sky?
I'd like to know 'bout lots of things
   And the true reason *why*.

Why?

Why do you make me eat the crust?
Of course, I'll eat it if I must,
But I don't like it much, because,
You see, my teeth aren't big like yours.

Why do you tell me not to shout
Whenever grown-ups are about?
I've often heard you laugh and sing
And make a noise like anything.

Why must I only have one sweet?
You know *you* think they're nice to eat,
And once – I watched you! – you took *eight*—
And, my, they *did* go at a rate!

Why must I often go to bed
Just when I want to play instead?
I can't *see* why I ought to, when
You sometimes stay up long past ten!

Where?

Where is that little pond I wish for?
Where are those little fish to fish for?

Where is my little rod for catching?
Where are the bites that I'll be scratching?

Where is my rusty reel for reeling?
Where is my trusty creel for creeling?

Where is the line for which I'm looking?
Where are those handy hooks for hooking?

Where is the worm I'll have to dig for?
Where are the boots that I'm too big for?

Where is there *any* boat for rowing?
Where is . . . ?
          Well, anyway, it's snowing.

                              David McCord

Who?

Who saw the smooth snow falling
All night long?
Who heard the white owl calling
Her strange, sad song?

Nobody.
Not anyone.
Not anyone at all.

Who heard the bleak wind howling
Over wild seas?
Who saw the starved form prowling
Through ghostly trees?

Nobody.
Not anyone.
Not anyone at all.

Nobody saw winter walking,
Nobody heard winter talking.

Nobody
Not anyone at all.

Leonard Clark

Who?

Who made the sky?
Who made the earth?
Who thought of my or anyone's birth?

Who made the stars?
Who made the moon?
Who thought of night or morning or noon?

Who made the bees?
Who made the grass?
Who made the bonnie wee laddie and lass?

Who made the sun?
Who made the rain?
Who thought of the horse's tail and mane?

Who made the trees?
Who made them tall?
Won't somebody tell me who made it all?

Jane Cattermull

The answers

'When did the world begin and how?'
I asked a lamb, a goat, a cow:

'What's it all about and why?'
I asked a hog as he went by:

'Where will the whole thing end, and when?'
I asked a duck, a goose, a hen:

And I copied all the answers too,
A quack, a honk, an oink, a moo.

Robert Clairmont

6
Riddles

1

What's in the church
But not the steeple?
The parson has it,
But not the people.

Answer: The letter 'r'.

2

Riddle me, riddle me, what is that—
Over the head and under the hat?

Answer: Hair.

3

As I was going to St Ives,
I met a man with seven wives:
Every wife had seven sacks;
Every sack had seven cats;
Every cat had seven kits.
Kits, cats, sacks, and wives—
How many were going to St Ives?

Answer: One. The others were coming from St Ives.

4

Two legs sat upon three legs,
With one leg in his lap;
In comes four legs,
And runs away with one leg.
Up jumps two legs,
Catches up three legs,
Throws it after four legs,
And makes him bring back one leg.

Answer: Four legs: a dog
Three legs: a stool
Two legs: a man
One leg: a leg of mutton

5

As I was going o'er yon moor of moss,
I met a man on a grey horse;
He whipped and he wailed.
I asked him what he ailed;
He said he was going to his father's funeral,
Who died seven years before he was born!

Answer: His father was a dyer.

6

Higher than a house, higher than a tree;
Oh! whatever can that be?

Answer: A star.

7

Black within, and red without,
Four corners round about.

8

A house full, a yard full,
And you can't catch a bowl full.

9

Which weighs heavier—
A stone of lead
Or a stone of feathers?

10

What do the children
In China call
Little yellow cats
When they are small?

11

My first is in milk but not in cream.
My second is in snooze, but not in dream.
My third is in us, but not in me.
My fourth is in grass but not in tree.
And my last is in everything, as fast as can be!
   What am I?

12

I'm called by the name of a man,
Yet am as little as a mouse;
When winter comes I love to be
With my red target near the house.

13

In marble walls as white as milk,
Lined with a skin as soft as silk,
Within a fountain crystal-clear
A golden apple doth appear.
No doors are there to this stronghold,
Yet thieves break in and steal the gold.

14

There was a little green house—
And in the little green house
There was a little brown house,
And in the little brown house
There was a little yellow house,
And in the little yellow house
There was a little white house,
And in the little white house
There was a little heart.

Answer: A walnut.

15

As white as milk,
And not milk;
As green as grass,
And not grass;
As red as blood,
And not blood;
As black as soot,
And not soot!

Answer: A bramble-blossom (look at one!).

16

Cut me, and I'll make you cry;
Cook me, and your tears will dry.

Ian Serraillier

Answer: An onion.

17

There is one that has a head without an eye,
And there's one that has an eye without a head.
You may find the answer if you try;
And when all is said,
Half the answer hangs upon a thread.

Christina Rossetti

Answer: A sewing needle.

18

Alive without breath,
As cold as death;
Never thirsty, ever drinking,
All in mail never clinking.

J. R. R. Tolkien

Answer: A fish.

19

I look at you
And you at me,
But are you really there?
For when I step
To right or left,
You are not anywhere.

Ian Serraillier

Answer: A mirror.

7
Picture-puzzle Fun

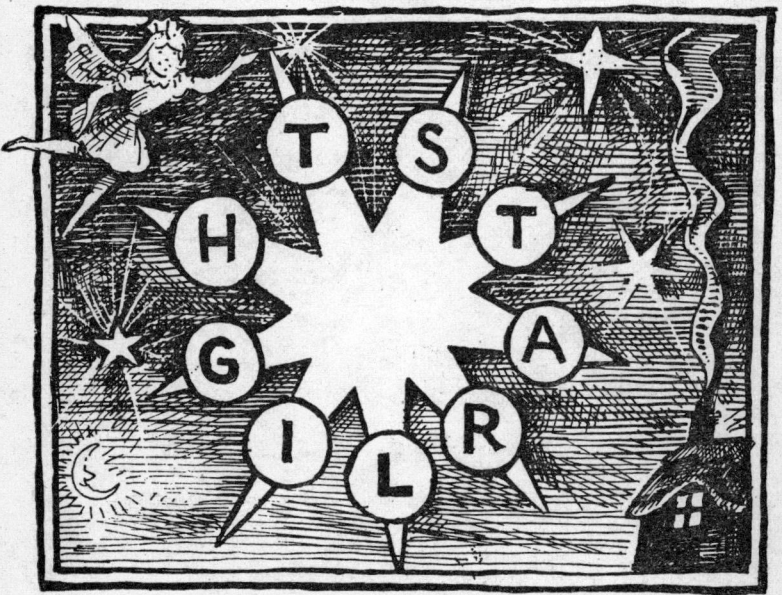

Starlight

Now 'Starlight' is the star which shines
    Upon the end of day;
It also is a super game,
    Which two or more can play!

You write each letter on a card
    Then shake them in a tin;
Each player has to draw the 'S'
    Before he can begin.

You have to spell 'Starlight' right through
   Until you reach the final 'T';
The first to make the word complete,
   The winner then shall be.

As a prize, they then will find
   The secret of 'Starlight';
The star will always make come true
   The wish they wish that night!

Michael Lisle

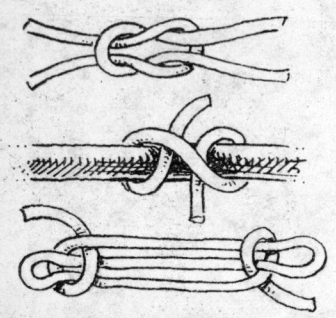 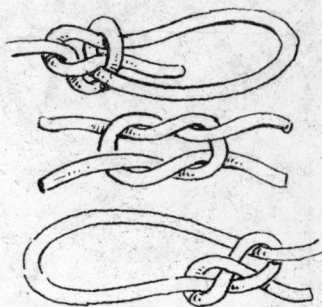

Tied in knots

Foam-flecked waves on coral strands,
Spices brought from distant lands;
A woolly creature nuzzling grass,
Children on a slide like glass;
A relation rather out of place,
A ribbon tied with skill and grace;
Each of these images you may find
Will bring a well-known knot to mind.

Marcia Armitage

Answer: Reef-knot, clove-hitch, sheepshank, slip-knot, granny knot, bowline.

54

A nursery rhyme puzzle

Can you fill up the gaps in these verses?
Each dot counts for one letter of a missing word.
It is easy if you study the pictures.

A *spider* scared a little girl.
And Tom a young *pig* stole.
A *pipe*, a *bowl*, and *fiddlers* three
Were called for by King Cole.

Two tumbled down *hill* when they went
For water in a *well*;
A mighty kingdom once was lost
For want of one small *nail*

Jungle calls and Brownie Sue

To gain her Discoverer Badge, young Sue
Thought she had better go to the Zoo.
But on reaching the place she was quite
    amazed—
Indeed, quite troubled and almost dazed.
The signposts had gone, and all was *noise*:
The SEA LIONS were shouting like eager boys.
Sue couldn't see DOVES, but she heard their
    sound;
ELEPHANTS' noises, too, were all around,
So she hurried away to the MONKEYS' home
And saw where LIONS and TIGERS roam.
The WOLVES gave a call that she could tell,
And she heard the PIGS grunting in their dell.
She listened hard to hear the SNAKES
And the funny noise that the big BEAR makes.
Brownie Sue found her way round the Zoo
By listening to animals – and won the badge too.

Rikki Taylor

Can you sort out the jumbled noises (below) that Sue heard and say to which animals they belong? 'SBRKA', for instance, turns out to be BARKS of sea-lions. Now try the others!

SNSGHII

ORSRA

RNIGMTPTUE

OWLSGR

HTCERNAIGT

OWLSGR

NASSLR

CSOO

SBRKA

Answer: CHATTERING of monkeys;
TRUMPETING of elephants;
BARKS of sea-lions;
ROARS of lions;
GRUNTS of pigs;
HOWLS of wolves;
SNARLS of tigers;
COOS of doves;
HISSING of snakes;
GROWLS of bears.

What's been stolen?

'Stop thief! Stop thief!' Policeman cries;
    Then he his whistle blows—
Running as quickly as he can
    After the thief he goes!

The items which the thief has stolen,
    He's hidden out of sight;
But you'll find them in the picture
    By looking at it right.

There are fourteen objects hidden,
    So search – both low and high;
The answer's given, but don't look
    Until you've had a try!

Michael Lisle

List of stolen objects: Cup, saucer, plate, egg-cup, knife, fork, spoon, necklace, comb, bracelet, clock, diamond ring, 50p coin, jug.

A puzzle poem

(Find the right names of all the sleepers on page 60)

I am a Slurriqe,
    I sleep in a tree,
Curled up in my tail
    As cosy can be.

I am a Tab,
   When the winter wind blows
I sleep in a barn
   Hung up by my toes!

I am a Doghegeh,
   In ditches I creep,
Find a warm hole there
   And roll up to sleep!

I am a Peque Paws,
   And snugly I hide
Under the ivy-leaves
   On the house-side.

I am a Gorf,
   And soundly I sleep
Upside down in the pond
   Where the water is deep.

I am a Dota,
   And I like to crawl
Beneath a damp stone
   Or under a wall.

And I am a Tribba,
   Who all winter through
Is just as awake
   And as lively as you!

Enid Blyton

8
Oh, Such Silliness

Oh, such silliness!

Oh, such silliness!
Silly willy-nilliness,
Dopey hillybilliness,
Rolling down the hilliness!

Oh, such craziness!
First of April Dayziness,
Giddy, goopy gayziness,
Bumpy dumb horseplayziness!

Oh, such sappiness!
Ridiculous slaphappiness,
Throw away his cappiness,
Jump into his lappiness!

Oh, such hilarity!
Falling down the stairity,
Tipping over chairity,
Shaving off your hairity!

Ghostliness and ghoulishness!
Push him in the poolishness,
Staying home from schoolishness—
Oh, such foolishness!

William Cole

My name is . . .

My name is Sluggery-wuggery
My name is Worms-for-tea
My name is Swallow-the-table-leg
My name is Drink-the-Sea.

My name is I-eat-saucepans
My name is I-like-snails
My name is Grand-piano-George
My name is I-ride-whales.

My name is Jump-the-chimney
My name is Bite-my-knee
My name is Jiggery-pokery
And Riddle-me-ree, and ME.

Pauline Clarke

On nicknames

Many nicknames
Are as common as glue:
Edward called Eddie,
Susan called Sue.

Now consider these questions:
Do you think that
The ferocious Bobcat
Is really a Robertcat?
The Bobolink, Robertolink?
I do. I do.

Perhaps you know
Where this verse is heading.
After I'm done
I'm going Robertsledding.

Louis Phillips

LMNTL

'Albert, have you a turtle?'
I'll say to him, and Bert'll
say 'Yes! Of *course* I have a turtle.'

But if I write,
'Have you a trtl, Albert?'
(as I might)
I wonder if Brtl guess
just what I mean?

We all have seen
a dog's tail wagl,
haven't we?
We all agree
that what a dogldo,
a polywogl too.

We've hrd a brd, grls gigl;
observed how skwrls hnt
for nuts; how big pigs grnt;
know how we feel
on hearing young pigsqweel.

Bbbbs buzz, and ktns play;
bats flitrfly azootowls cry.
Why don't we *spell* that way?
Make ibx look like gnu?
Lfnts too; zbras inizoo?
I do. Do you?

David McCord

Rhyme for a simpleton

I said, 'This horse, sir, will you shoe?'
    And soon the horse was shod.
I said, 'This deed, sir, will you do?'
    And soon the deed was dod!

I said, 'This stick, sir, will you break?'
    At once the stick he broke.
I said, 'This coat, sir, will you make?'
    And soon the coat he moke!

Scat! Scitten!

Even though
 a cat has a kitten,
 not a rat has a ritten,
 not a bat has a bitten,
 not a gnat has a gnitten,
 not a sprat has a spritten.
 That is that – that is thitten.

David McCord

I always get things right

In Backwards Land
Cats go 'Woem'
& dogs 'Wow Bow,'
Cows go 'Oom'
& ducks go 'Kcauq.'
An entire barnyard
Backward baying,
But you'll never see me
That like anything saying.

Louis Phillips

If things grew down

If things grew down
Instead of up,
A dog would grow
Into a pup.
A cat would grow
Into a kitten.
Your sweater would grow
Into a mitten.
A cow would grow
Into a calf
And a whole would grow
Into a half.
Big would grow
Into something small
And small would grow
Into nothing at all.

Robert D. Hoeft

As I was going out one day

As I was going out one day
My head fell off and rolled away.
But when I saw that it was gone,
I picked it up and put it on.

And when I got into the street
A fellow cried: 'Look at your feet!'
I looked at them and sadly said:
'I've left them both asleep in bed!'

Somebody

Somebody being a nobody,
Thinking to look like a somebody,
Said that he thought me a nobody:
Good little somebody-nobody,
Had you not known me a somebody,
Would you have called me a nobody?

Alfred, Lord Tennyson

The Hidebehind

Have you seen the Hidebehind?
I don't think you will, mind you,
because as you're running through the dark
the Hidebehind's behind you.

Michael Rosen

Posers

Supposing you had 6 baboons,
   And made them dance a dozen jigs,
How many pairs of pantaloons
   Would equal 50 sucking-pigs?

If every house had 7 roofs,
   And every roof 1000 tiles,
How much is worn off horses' hoofs
   In trotting 20 000 miles?

If 60 stockings made a pair,
　And all our hats were worn in twos,
How many braces should we wear,
　Including slippers, boots, and shoes?

If 20 kittens made a pie
　Of half a 100 mouses' tails,
How far is Rome from Peckham Rye
　Before the equinoctial gales?

If 40 snails could crawl a mile
　In ½ the time it takes to wink,
How many pills would cure the bile?—
　Please work it out in pen and ink.

If 7 double-barrelled guns
　Killed 80 rabbits in an hour,
How many pounds of hot-cross-buns
　Could Jumbo in a day devour?

If every dog had 50 barks,
　And every bark 11 bites,
How many children's Noah's Arks
　Would equal 2 electric lights?

If 30 chimney-pots of ale,
　And ½ a looking-glass of wine,
Were all reduced to smallest scale,
　What is it multiplied by 9?

If 7 senses are confused
　By whales 600 acres long,
Why shouldn't people be amused
　At this my idiotic song?

　　　　　　　　　　　　　　X. Parke

9
Word-scrambling and Tongue-twisting

1

The bottle of perfume that Willie sent
Was highly displeasing to Millicent.
   Her thanks were so cold
   That they quarrelled, I'm told,
Through that silly scent Willie sent Millicent.

2

Betty Botter bought some butter,
   But she said, 'My butter's bitter.
If I put it in my batter
   It will make my batter bitter.
If I buy some better butter
   It will make my batter better.'
So she bought some better butter
   And it made her batter better.

3

A twister of twists once twisted a twist;
The twist that he twisted was a three-twisted twist.
If in twisting the twist, one twist should untwist,
The untwisted twist would untwist the twist.

4

A tutor who taught on the flute
Tried to teach two young tooters to toot.
    Said the two to the tutor,
    'Is it harder to toot, or
To tutor two tooters to toot?'

5

Peter Piper picked a peck of pickled pepper
    Off a pewter plate;
A peck of pickled pepper Peter Piper picked
    Off a pewter plate;
If Peter Piper picked a peck of pickled pepper
    Off a pewter plate;
Where's the peck of pickled pepper Peter Piper
    picked
    Off a pewter plate?

6

How many cans can a cannibal nibble
  If a cannibal can nibble cans?
As many cans as a cannibal can nibble
  If a cannibal can nibble cans.

7

When he killed the Mudjekeewis,
Of the skin he made him mittens;
Made them with the fur side inside,
Made them with the skin side outside.
He, to get the warm side inside,
Put the inside skin side outside;
He, to get the cold side outside,
Put the warm side fur side inside.
That's why he put fur side inside,
Why he put the skin side outside,
Why he turned them inside outside.

8

A flea and a fly in a flue
Were imprisoned, so what could they do?
   Said the fly, 'Let us flee.'
   Said the flea, 'Let us fly.'
So they flew through a flaw in the flue.

9

I saw Esau Wood saw wood
Esau Wood's wood-saw sawed his wood
Said he saw his saw saw
If Esau's wood-saw saws his wood
Would Esau's wood-saw saw wood-saws?

Michael Rosen

10

$2 +$ $=$

Whatever one toucan can do
is sooner done by toucans two,
and three toucans (it's very true)
can do much more than two can do.

And toucans numbering two plus two can
manage more than all the zoo can.
In short, there is no toucan who can
do what four or three or two can.

Jack Prelutsky

10
All Shapes and Sizes

A cello

My cello big and fat
makes
the sound
of a screeching
rat. It plays F
double sharp
when I want
it to play
B flat. It
sounds like
a bad com-
position when
I play in the 4th
position. If I try
to play vibrato my
bow goes all
s - t - a - c - c -
ato
!

Richard Lester

Summer moon

She goes
Silently at the full
The moon in her summer sky.
And sleeping villages are white as winter's snows,
Tall chimneys, black canals and shadowy streets look very beautiful.
But when each night I watch her calmly wandering by
I hope that sometimes, as her roundness glows,
A gold eye, vast and wonderful,
She will see my
Little eye.

Leonard Clark

Diamond cut diamond

Two cats
One up a tree
One under the tree
The cat up a tree is he
The cat under the tree is she
The tree is witch elm, just incidentally.
He takes no notice of she, she takes no notice of he.
He stares at the woolly clouds passing, she stares at the tree.
There's been a lot written about cats, by Old Possum, Yeats and Company
But not Alfred de Musset or Lord Tennyson or Poe or anybody
Wrote about one cat under, and one cat up, a tree.
God knows why this should be left for me
Except I like cats as cats be
Especially one cat up
And one cat under
A witch elm
Tree.

Ewart Milne

Seal

See how he dives
  From the rocks with a zoom!
  See how he darts
    Through his watery room
    Past crabs and eels
      And green seaweed,
        Past fluffs of sandy
        Minnow feed!
      See how he swims
      With a swerve and a twist,
  A flip of the flipper,
  A flick of the wrist!
Quicksilver-quick,
Softer than spray,
Down he plunges
And sweeps away;
Before you can think,
Before you can utter
Words like 'Dill pickle'
Or 'Apple butter',
  Back up he swims
    Past sting-ray and shark,
    Out with a zoom,
    A whoop, a bark;
      Before you can say
      Whatever you wish,
        He plops at your side
        With a mouthful of fish!

William Jay Smith

76

The mouse's tale

Fury said to a
  mouse, That he
   met in the
   house,
    'Let us
     both go to
     law: *I* will
     prosecute
     you. Come,
    I'll take no
   denial; We
   must have a
   trial: For
  really this
  morning I've
nothing
to do.'
said the
 mouse to the
 cur, 'Such
  a trial,
   dear Sir,
   With
    no jury
     or judge,
     would be
     wasting
    our
    breath.'
    'I'll be
   judge, I'll
  be jury,'
 Said
 cunning
 old Fury:
 'I'll
   try the
   whole
    cause,
   and
   condemn
  you
 to
death.'

Lewis Carroll

Earth-worm

Do
you
squirm
when
you
see
an earth-worm?
I never
do squirm
because I think
a big fat worm
is really rather clever
the way it can shrink
and go
so small
without
a sound
into the ground.
And then
what about
all
that
work it does
and no oxygen
or miner's hat?
Marvellous
you have to admit.
even if you don't like fat

How will that

thin
slippery skin
it makes its way
day after day
through the soil,
such honest toil.
And don't forget
the dirt
it eats, I bet
you wouldn't like to come out
at night to squirt
it all over the place
with no eyes in your face:
I doubt
too if you know
an earth-worm is deaf, but
it can hear YOU go
to and fro
even if you cut
it in half.
So
do not laugh
or squirm
again
when
you
suddenly
see
a worm.   *Leonard Clark*

The crinoline

In days
long gone
our grandmas
quaint   Set
all   the   world
a-grin   By
d o n n i n g
when   they
wore   their
paint, The bulky
crinoline.   They
waddled in the park and
town Like portions of
balloons, Or monster egg-
cups upside down. Or cut-in-
two cocoons; They blocked the
roadway and the lane, Their bulki-
ness was such; Likewise they distant kept a swain Who strove a waist
to clutch. They whirled about in every
breeze And wobbled in the gale, Till
timid men went on their knees In apprehen-
sion pale. In play-house or in con-
cert-hall, In vestibule or stair, They
pushed the males towards the wall And kept
them tightly there. The drawing-room they
crammed and jammed; They blocked the cab and
'bus. Until the public loudly damned Their
plaguey overplus; And while the curs-ed crinoline The heart of mankind vexed, A voice arose
from out the din 'What next? O, Lord, what next?'

E. G. Murphy

Exactly like a 'V'

When my brother Tommy
Sleeps in bed with me
He doubles up
And makes
himself
exactly
like
a
V

And 'cause the bed is not so wide
A part of him is on my side.

Abram Bunn Ross

11

Poems That
Run Off the
Page

Failure

I'm trying to write the longest first line that poetry has
    ever had.
For a start that wasn't bad;
Now here comes a longer oneeeeeeeeeeeeeeeeeeeeeeeee
I know I cheated:
It was the only way I could avoid being defeated.

Spike Milligan

Banananananananananananananananananananana

I thought I'd win the spelling bee
    And get right to the top,
But I started to spell 'banana',
    And I didn't know when to stop.

William Cole

Pantomime poem

'HE'S BEHIND YER!'
chorused the children
but the warning came too late.

The monster leaped forward
and fastening its teeth into his neck,
tore off the head.

The body fell to the floor
'MORE' cried the children

'MORE, MORE, MORE

MORE

MORE

MORE

MORE

Roger McGough

I woke up this morning

I woke up this morning
At quarter past seven.
I kicked up the covers
And stuck out my toe.
And ever since then
(That's a quarter past seven)
They haven't said anything
Other than 'no.'
They haven't said anything
Other than 'Please, dear,
Don't do what you're doing,'
Or 'Lower your voice.'
Whatever I've done
And however I've chosen,
I've done the wrong thing
And I've made the wrong choice.
I didn't wash well
And I didn't say thank you.
I didn't shake hands
And I didn't say please
I didn't say sorry
When passing the candy,

I banged the box into
Miss Witelson's knees.
I didn't say sorry.
I didn't stand straighter.
I didn't speak louder
When asked what I'd said.
Well, I said
That tomorrow
At quarter past seven
They can
Come in and get me.
I'm Staying In Bed.

12
Sing, Dance and Go Rum Boom Boom!

Singing game

In this game one person plays the Farmer and the others join hands and dance round him singing:

There was a farmer had a dog,
  His name was Bobby Bingo.
B-I-N-G-O, B-I-N-G-O, B-I-N-G-O,
  His name was Bobby Bingo.

Now the circle of players stand still and
the Farmer points to one person,
who calls: B
   the next, who calls: I
     the next, who calls: N
       the next, who calls: G
         the next, who calls: O,
who now becomes the Farmer.
Then everyone sings:

   And Bingo was his name!

The game is then repeated.

Clap your hands

(Sing to the tune of Jingle Bells: *the actions*
should be obvious!)

Clap your hands! Clap your hands!
This is how it's done.
Slap your knees! Slap your knees!
Now you're having fun.
Stamp your feet! Stamp your feet!
Make a lot of noise.
Because we want the world to share
In all our Scouting joys.

         Colin McKay

Another singing game

This time everyone must sit on the floor in a circle. The name of a musical instrument (such as BUGLE HORN) is given to each player, who must imitate that instrument whenever it is mentioned. Everyone joins in to sing the rhyme, though the sounds indicated in CAPITAL LETTERS must be made by the person chosen for the particular instrument. It is also a good idea to ask someone to be the Conductor, whose job it is to make sure the appropriate instrument comes in 'on time'.

We can play the Big Bass Drum,
　　And this is the music to it:
RUM BOOM BOOM goes the Big Bass Drum,
　　And this is the way to do it.

We can play on the Bugle Horn,
　　And this is the music to it:
TA TA TARAH goes the Bugle Horn,
RUM BOOM BOOM goes the Big Bass Drum,
　　And this is the way to do it.

We can play on the Double Bass,
  And this is the music to it:
ZOOM ZOOM ZOOM goes the Double Bass,
TA TA TARAH goes the Bugle Horn,
RUM BOOM BOOM goes the Big Bass Drum,
  And this is the way to do it.

We can play on the Tambourine,
  And this is the music to it:
JING A TING TING goes the Tambourine,
ZOOM ZOOM ZOOM goes the Double Bass,
TA TA TARAH goes the Bugle Horn,
RUM BOOM BOOM goes the Big Bass Drum,
  And this is the way to do it.

A new instrument is added to each verse, until you end up with:

We can play on the little Flute,
    And this is the music to it:
TOOTLE TOOTLE TOOT goes the little Flute,
MEENY MINN MINN goes the Violin,
RUMA TUM TUM goes the Kettle Drum,
PLOM PLIM PLOM goes the Old Banjo,
TICKA TICKA TECK go the Castanets,
JING A TING TING goes the Tambourine,
ZOOM ZOOM ZOOM goes the Double Bass,
TA TA TARAH goes the Bugle Horn,
RUM BOOM BOOM goes the Big Bass Drum,

Everyone:

AND THIS IS THE WAY TO DO IT!

The stolen gong song

(*) means when you should clap two pieces of wood together

Charlie
Wong (*)
Stole
my
gong (*) (*)

Piers Davies

(The next five poems can all be read aloud and, for greater fun, a friend can make the 'noise sounds' of the words in CAPITAL LETTERS.)

Rhyme for moles

Ring-a-ring-a-molehills,
A pocketful of fat worms,
    ATISHOO! ATISHOO!
    We all dig down.

In and out the grass roots
Underneath the meadows,
    ATISHOO! ATISHOO!
    We all move along.

Velvet fur and whiskers,
Tunnels by the morning.
    ATISHOO! ATISHOO!
    We all come up.

Leonard Clark

Clickity-click!

Needles knit,
CLICKITY-CLICK!
Twisting the wool
Making a stitch.
CLICK-KNIT!
FLICK-KNIT!
Making a sweater
SPLITTERY-SLICK!

Swish goes the broomstick!

There was an old witch,
Believe it if you can,
Who tapped at the window
And who ran-ran-ran.

She ran helter-skelter,
With her toes in the air,
Cornstalks flying
From her old witchy hair.

SWISH! went her broomstick,
MEOW! went her cat,
PLOP! went her hop-toad
Sitting on her hat.

'WEE!' chuckled she,
'HI-DEE-HO-HI!'
Hallowe'en night
When witches fly!

'WEE!'

This is the way they ride

This is the way the ladies ride,
    TRI, TRE, TRE, TREE,
    TRI, TRE, TRE, TREE;
This is the way the ladies ride,
    TRI, TRE, TRE, TRE, TRI-TRE-TRE-TREE!

This is the way the gentlemen ride,
    GALLOP-A-TROT,
    GALLOP-A-TROT;
This is the way the gentlemen ride,
    GALLOP-A-GALLOP-A-TROT!

This is the way the farmers ride,
    HOBBLEDY-HOY,
    HOBBLEDY-HOY;
This is the way the farmers ride,
    HOBBLEDY HOBBLEDY-HOY!

John Cook

John Cook he had a little grey mare,
   HEE, HAW, HUM;
Her legs were long and her back was bare,
   HEE, HAW, HUM;
John Cook was riding up Shooter's Bank,
   HEE, HAW, HUM;
The mare she began to kick and to prank,
   HEE, HAW, HUM;
John Cook was riding up Shooter's Hill,
   HEE, HAW, HUM;
His mare fell down and made her will,
   HEE, HAW, HUM;
The bridle and saddle were laid on the shelf,
   HEE, HAW, HUM;
If you want any more you must sing it yourself,
   HEE, HAW, HUM.

Wow! wow! wow!

(To be recited by one person, with two or more friends making the sounds of the Chorus.)

Speak roughly to your little boy,
   And beat him when he sneezes:
He only does it to annoy,
   Because he knows it teases.

Chorus
WOW! WOW! WOW!

I speak severely to my boy,
  I beat him when he sneezes;
For he can thoroughly enjoy
  The pepper when he pleases!

Chorus
WOW! WOW! WOW!

Lewis Carroll

Here *is the sea*

(a finger game)

Here is the sea, the wavy sea.
Here is the boat and here is me.

Use one hand to make wave movements.
Hold the other hand in a fist over the waves.
It's the boat. Pop up the thumb to be 'me'.

And the little fishes down below
Wiggle their tails and away they go.

Stop making waves and wiggle your fingers
as if they were the fish under the boat.
Gliding and swerving, swim the fish-fingers
away.

Who teaches her young to snatch and grab?
None other than nippity Mumma Crab.

Jean Chapman

Dance, Thumbkin, dance

(another finger game)

Dance, Thumbkin, dance;
　　　　　(move thumb)

Dance, you merrymen, everyone.
　　　　　(move all fingers)

For Thumbkin, he can dance alone,
　　　　　(move thumb alone)

Thumbkin, he can dance alone.
　　　　　(move thumb alone)

Dance, Foreman, dance,
　　　　　(move first finger)

Dance, you merrymen, everyone.
　　　　　(move all fingers)

But Foreman, he can dance alone,
        (move first finger)

Foreman, he can dance alone.
        (move first finger)

Dance, Longman, dance,
        (move second finger)

Dance, you merrymen, everyone.
        (move all fingers)

For Longman, he can dance alone,
        (move second finger)

Longman, he can dance alone.
        (move second finger)

Dance, Ringman, dance,
        (move third finger)

Dance, you merrymen, dance.
        (move all fingers)

But Ringman cannot dance alone,
        (move third finger)

Ringman, he cannot dance alone.
        (move third finger)

Dance, Littleman, dance,
        (move fourth finger)

Dance, you merrymen, dance.
        (move all fingers)

But Littleman, he can dance alone,
        (move fourth finger)

Littleman, he can dance alone.
        (move fourth finger)

*(The following four poems can be made even
more exciting by being read aloud at different
speeds and rhythms – in the next two verses, for
instance, imagine you are travelling on an old
steam train of long ago as it goes clickety-clack,
clickety-clack over the railway lines.)*

From a railway carriage

Faster than fairies, faster than witches,
Bridges and houses, hedges and ditches;
And charging along like troops in a battle,
All through the meadows the horses and cattle:
All of the sights of the hill and the plain
Fly as thick as driving rain;
And ever again, in the wink of an eye,
Painted stations whistle by.

Here is a child who clambers and scrambles,
All by himself and gathering brambles;
Here is a tramp who stands and gazes,
And there is the green for stringing the daisies!
Here is a cart run away in the road
Lumping along with man and load;
And here is a mill, and there is a river:
Each a glimpse and gone for ever!

Robert Louis Stevenson

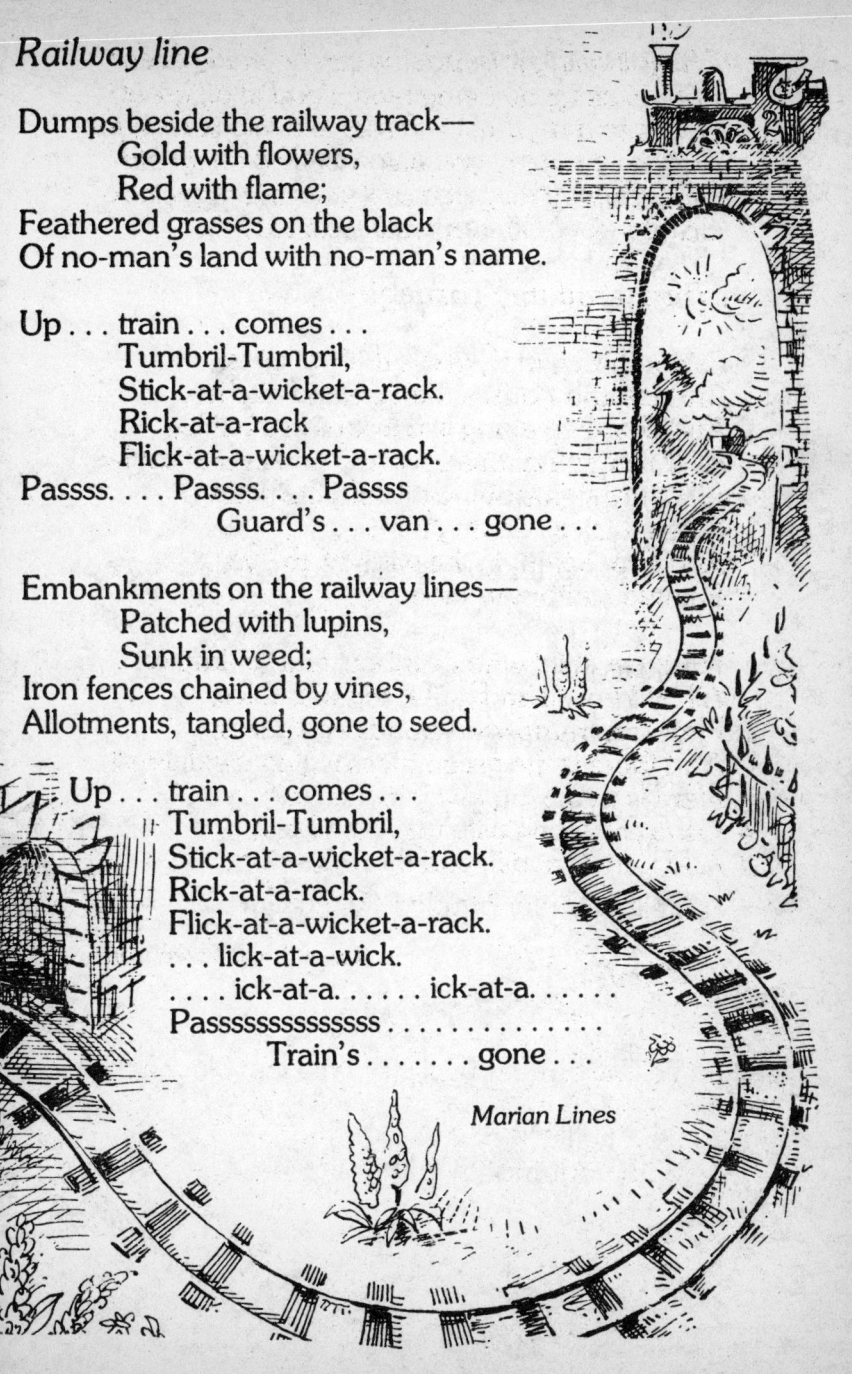

Railway line

Dumps beside the railway track—
      Gold with flowers,
      Red with flame;
Feathered grasses on the black
Of no-man's land with no-man's name.

Up . . . train . . . comes . . .
      Tumbril-Tumbril,
      Stick-at-a-wicket-a-rack.
      Rick-at-a-rack
      Flick-at-a-wicket-a-rack.
Passss. . . . Passss. . . . Passss
          Guard's . . . van . . . gone . . .

Embankments on the railway lines—
      Patched with lupins,
      Sunk in weed;
Iron fences chained by vines,
Allotments, tangled, gone to seed.

Up . . . train . . . comes . . .
      Tumbril-Tumbril,
      Stick-at-a-wicket-a-rack.
      Rick-at-a-rack.
      Flick-at-a-wicket-a-rack.
      . . . lick-at-a-wick.
      . . . . ick-at-a. . . . . ick-at-a. . . . . .
      Passssssssssssss . . . .
          Train's . . . . gone . . .

Marian Lines

A thrush's song

Did he do it? Did he do it?
Come and see, come and see,
Cherry sweet, cherry sweet,
Knee-deep, knee-deep,
Pity you, pity you,
To me! To me! To me!

Pamela Tennant

Yellow butter

Yellow butter purple jelly red jam black bread

Spread it thick
Say it quick

Yellow butter purple jelly red jam black bread

Spread it thicker
Say it quicker

Yellow butter purple jelly red jam black bread

Now repeat it
While you eat it

Yellow butter purple jelly red jam black bread

Don't talk
With your mouth full!

Mary Ann Hoberman

13
Fun With Numbers

Numbers

There are Hundreds of Numbers. They mount
    up so high,
That if you could count every star in the sky
From the Tail of the Bear to the Waterman's Hat,
There still would be even more Numbers than
    that!

There are Thousands of Numbers. So many
    there be,
That if you could count every drop in the sea
From the Mexican Gulf to the Lincolnshire Flat,
There still would be even more Numbers than
    that!

There are Millions of Numbers. So many to
    spare,
That if you could count every insect in air,
The moth, the mosquito, the bee, and the gnat,
There still would be even more Numbers than
    that!

There's no end to Numbers! But don't be afraid!
There only are Ten out of which they are made,
Learn from Nought up to Nine, and the rest will
    come pat,
For the Numbers of Numbers all come out of
    that!

Eleanor Farjeon

$$1 + 1 = 2$$

1 and 1 are 2—
That's for me and you.

2 and 2 are 4—
That's a couple more.

3 and 3 are 6
Barley-sugar sticks.

4 and 4 are 8
Tumblers at the gate.

5 and 5 are 10
Bluff seafaring men.

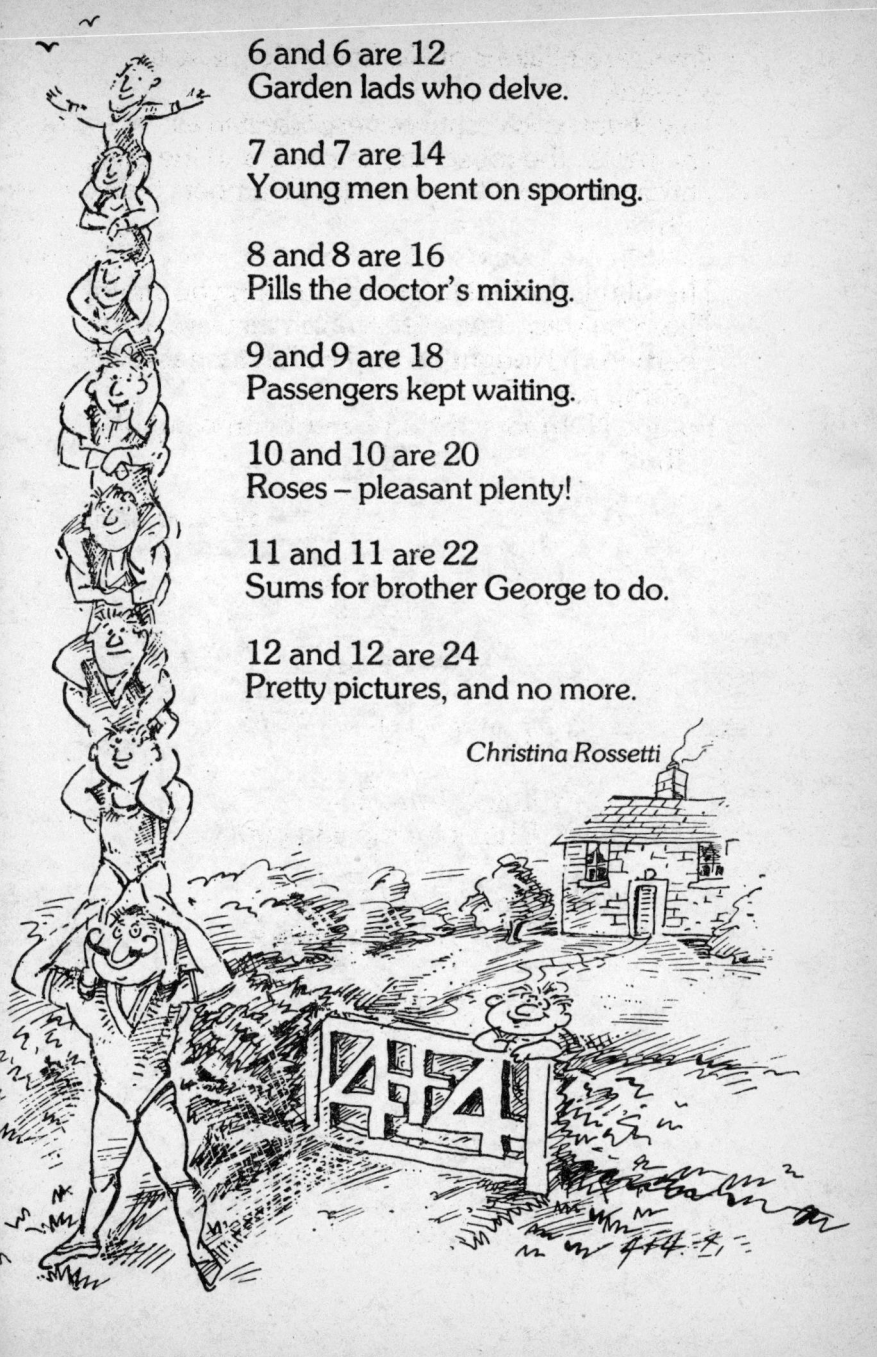

6 and 6 are 12
Garden lads who delve.

7 and 7 are 14
Young men bent on sporting.

8 and 8 are 16
Pills the doctor's mixing.

9 and 9 are 18
Passengers kept waiting.

10 and 10 are 20
Roses – pleasant plenty!

11 and 11 are 22
Sums for brother George to do.

12 and 12 are 24
Pretty pictures, and no more.

Christina Rossetti

One

One, he loves; two, he loves;
Three, he loves, they say;
Four, he loves with all his heart;
Five, he casts away.
Six, he loves; seven, she loves;
Eight, they both love.
Nine, he comes; ten, he tarries;
Eleven, he courts; twelve, he marries.

One, two

One, two,
Buckle my shoe;
Three, four,
Knock at the door;
Five, six,
Pick up sticks;
Seven, eight,
Lay them straight;
Nine, ten,
A good fat hen.
Eleven, twelve,
Dig and delve;
Thirteen, fourteen,
Maids a-courting;
Fifteen, sixteen,
Maids a-kissing;
Seventeen, eighteen,
Maids a-waiting;
Nineteen, twenty,
My stomach's empty.

One, two, three

One, two, three, me mother caught a flea,
She put it in the tea-pot
To make a cup of tea.
The flea jumped out,
Me mother gave a shout,
And in came a copper
With his shirt hanging out.

One, two, three, four

One . . . two!
Kittens that mew.
Two . . . three!
Birds on a tree.
Three . . . four!
Frog at the door.
Four . . . five!
Bees from a hive.
Five . . . six!
Puppy dog licks.
Six . . . seven!
Stars in heaven.
Seven . . . eight!
A golden plate.
Eight . . . nine!
Ducks in a line.
Nine . . . ten!
Start again.

One, two, three, four, five

One, two, three, four, five,
Once I caught a fish alive;
Six, seven, eight, nine, ten,
Then I let it go again.

Why did you let it go?
Because it bit my finger so.
Which finger did it bite?
This little finger on the right.

Six

When I was One,
I had just begun.

When I was Two,
I was nearly new.

When I was Three,
I was hardly Me.

When I was Four,
I was not much more.

When I was Five,
I was just alive.

But now I am Six, I'm as clever as clever,
So I think I'll be six now for ever and ever.

A. A. Milne

Rain before seven

Rain before seven,
Clear by eleven.

The dream of a boy
who lived at Nine Elms

Nine grenadiers, with bayonets in their guns;
Nine bakers' baskets, with hot-cross buns;
Nine brown elephants, standing in a row;
Nine new bicycles, good ones to go;
Nine knickerbocker suits, with buttons all
      complete;
Nine pairs of skates with straps for the feet;
Nine clever conjurors eating hot coals;
Nine sturdy mountaineers leaping on their poles;
Nine little drummer-boys beating on their
      drums;
Nine fat aldermen sitting on their thumbs;
Nine new knockers to our front door;
Nine new neighbours that I never saw before;
Nine times running I dreamt it all plain;
With bread and cheese for supper I could dream
      it all again!

William Brighty Rands

Ten little chickadees

Ten little chickadees sitting on a line,
One flew away and then there were nine.

Nine little chickadees on a farmer's gate,
One flew away and then there were eight.

Eight little chickadees looking up to heaven,
One flew away and then there were seven.

Seven little chickadees gathering up sticks,
One flew away and then there were six.

Six little chickadees learning how to dive,
One flew away and then there were five.

Five little chickadees sitting at a door,
One flew away and then there were four.

Four little chickadees could not agree,
One flew away and then there were three.

Three little chickadees looking very blue,
One flew away and then there were two.

Two little chickadees sitting in the sun,
One flew away and then there was one.

One little chickadee living all alone,
He flew away and then there was NONE!

Fifteen seconds

If you don't put your shoes on before I count
   fifteen
then we won't go to the woods to climb the
   chestnut one
        But I can't find them
Two
        I can't
They're under the sofa three
        No
        O yes
Four five six
        Stop – they've got knots they've got
          knots
You should untie the laces when you take your
   shoes off seven
        Will you do one shoe while I do the
          other then?
Eight but that would be cheating
        Please
All right
        It always . . .
Nine
        It always sticks – I'll use my teeth
Ten
        It won't it won't
        It has – look.
Eleven
        I'm not wearing any socks
Twelve
        Stop counting stop counting. Mum
          where are my socks mum
They're in your shoes. Where you left them.
        I didn't

Thirteen

       O they're inside out and upside down
         and bundled up

Fourteen

       Have you done the knot on the shoe
       you were . . .

Yes

Put it on the right foot

       But socks don't have right and wrong
         foot

The shoes silly

Fourteen and a half

       I am I am. Wait.
       Don't go to the woods without me
       Look that's one shoe already

Fourteen and threequarters

       There

You haven't tied the bows yet

       We could do them on the way there

No we won't fourteen and seven eighths

       Help me then
       You know I'm not fast at bows

Fourteen and fifteen sixteeeenths

       A single bow is all right isn't it

Fifteen we're off.

       See I did it.
       Didn't I?

Michael Rosen

Counting rhyme

One, Two,
Haven't a clue;
Three, Four,
Ask for more;
Five, Six,
Fiddlesticks;
Seven, Eight,
Get it straight;
Nine, Ten,
Please say when;
Eleven, Twelve,
Better shelve;
Thirteen, Fourteen,
I'm going courting;
Fifteen, Sixteen,
Kathleen Mavourneen,
Seventeen, Eighteen,
Fascinating;
Nineteen, Twenty,
And that's plenty.

Charles Connell

Arithmetic

Arithmetic is where numbers fly like pigeons in
    and out of your head.
Arithmetic tells you how many you lose or win if
    you know how many you had before you lost
    or won.
Arithmetic is seven eleven all good children go to
    heaven – or five six bundle of sticks.

Arithmetic is numbers you squeeze from your head to your hand to your pencil to your paper till you get the answer.

Arithmetic is where the answer is right and everything is nice and you can look out of the window and see the blue sky – or the answer is wrong and you have to start all over and try again and see how it comes out this time.

If you take a number and double it and double it again and then double it a few more times, the number gets bigger and bigger and goes higher and higher and only arithmetic can tell you what the number is when you decide to quit doubling.

Arithmetic is where you have to multiply – and you carry the multiplication table in your head and hope you won't lose it.

If you have two animal crackers, one good and one bad, and you eat one and a striped zebra with streaks all over him eats the other, how many animal crackers will you have if somebody offers you five six seven and you say No no no and you say Nay nay nay and you say Nix nix nix?

If you ask your mother for one fried egg for breakfast and she gives you two fried eggs and you eat both of them, who is better in arithmetic, you or your mother?

Carl Sandburg

Multiplication

Multiplication is vexation,
Division is as bad;
The Rule of Three it puzzles me,
And fractions drive me mad.

Crazy arithmetic

4 in 2 goes twice as fast,
   If 2 and 4 change places;
But how can 2 and 3 make four,
   If 3 and 2 make faces?

D'Arcy Wentworth Thompson

14
Alphabet
Fun

As simple as ABC

A, B, C,
D, E, F, G,
H, I, J, K, if you look you'll see;
L, M, N, O, P, Q,
R, S, T, U, V, W,
X, Y, Z.

The alphabet

A, B, C, and D,
Pray, playmates, agree.
E, F, and G,
Well, so it shall be.
J, K, and L,
In peace we will dwell.
M, N, and O,
To play let us go.
P, Q, R, and S,
Love may we possess.
W, X, and Y,
Will not quarrel and die.
Z, and ampersand,
Go to school at command.

Tea at the farm

A, B, C, D,
   E, F, G.
Baby and her teddy bear
   Going out to tea.

H, I, J, K,
   L, M, N.
Seven little fluffy chicks,
   One big speckled hen.

O, P, Q, and
   R, S, T.
Lots of yellow buttercups,
   One brown honey bee.

U, V, W,
   X, Y, Z.
Baby and her teddy bear
   Going home to bed!

One alphabet

A stands for the Apple that grew on the tree.
B was the Boat that would hold you and me.
C was the Cat that caught all the mice.
D was the Doll dressed up very nice.
E was the Eagle and chained to the perch.
F stands for Fanny returning from church.
G was the Gardener a-working many hours.
H was the Hothouse that held his choice flowers.
I was the Indian with his arrow and bow.
J was the Jackdaw I very well know.
K was the Keeper who fed the wild beasts.
L was the Lion and none of the least.
M was the Magpie who could say all it heard.
N noisy Nancy who would have the last word.
O was the Ostler whose horse was his pride.
P was the Pony that William could ride.
Q was the Queen dressed up all so grand.
R was the Rabbit that fed from her hand.
S was the Ship that was laden with gold.
T was the Turk who was warlike and bold.
U was my Uncle with his new umberello.
V was the Valet quite a complaisant fellow.
W was the Welshman just returned from Wales.
X was the shape of a windmill's four sails.
Y was the Youth who could bear with a grace.
Z the New Zealander with his fine figured face.

Another alphabet

A was an Archer who shot at a frog;
B was a Butcher who had a great dog.
C was a Captain all covered with lace;
D was a Drummer who played with grace.
E was an Esquire with pride in his brow;
F was a Farmer who followed a plough.
G was a Gamester who had but ill luck;
H was a Hunter who hunted a buck.
I was an Italian who had a white mouse;
J was a Joiner and built up a house.
K was a King so mighty and grand;
L was a Lady who had a white hand.
M was a Miser who hoarded up gold;
N was a Nobleman gallant and bold.
O was an Oyster Girl and went about town;
P was a Parson and wore a black gown.
Q was a Queen who wore a silk slip;
R was a Robber who wanted a whip.
S was a Sailor who spent all he got;
T was a Tinker who mended a pot.
U was an Usher with dunces severe;
V was a Veteran who never knew fear.
W was a Watchman and guarded the door;
X was expensive and so became poor.
Y was a Youth who did not like school;
Z was a Zany, a poor harmless fool.

A was an apple-pie

A was an apple-pie
B bit it, C cut it, D dealt it,
E enjoyed it, F fought for it,
G got it, H hoped for it,
I inquired about it,
J jumped on it, K kept it,
L longed for it, M mourned for it,
N nodded at it, O opened it,
P peeped in it, Q quartered it,
R ran for it, S sat on it, T took it,
U upset it, V viewed it, W wanted it,
X crossed it, Y yearned for it,
And Z put it in his pocket, and said:
'Well done!'

To a Mr Wellwood who exaggerated

You double each story you tell,
    You double each sight that you see;
Your name's W.E. double L,
    W, double O, D.

W

The King he sent for his wise men all
    To find a rhyme for W;
When they had thought a good long time
But could not think of a single rhyme,
    'I'm sorry,' said he, 'to trouble you.'

James Reeves

Double-U

Heigh ho! my heart is low,
  My mind is all on one;
It's W for I know Who,
  And T for my love, Tom!

L, T, H, B

L stands for London
T stands for Town
H stands for Harry
and B stands for Brown.

Harry Brown of London Town
Said he'd marry me.
And isn't it a blessing
To sit on Harry's knee?

The vowels

We are very little creatures,
All of different voice and features;
One of us in glAss is set,
One of us you'll find in jEt,
T'other you may see in tIn,
And the fourth a bOx within.
If the fifth you would pursue,
It can never fly from yoU.

Jonathan Swift

What's your name?

When they said
'What's your name?'
I used to say,
'Michael Rosen
Rosen
R, O, S, E, N
with a silent "Q" as in rhubarb.'

and they'd say,
'That's not very funny.'

Michael Rosen

15
Well I Never!

A blink

A blink, I think, is the same as a wink,
A blink is a wink that grew,
For a *wink* you wink with only one eye,
And a *blink* you wink with two!

Jacqueline Segal

A house without children

A house without children
is like a tree without birds
says the old proverb.

The house was full of birds—
budgerigars, canaries,
goldfinches – a dazzling
deafening family

raised by my aunt and uncle.
I went to stay with them
one summer holiday.

And they said a footprint
here and there, the odd chatter
was all right: but not, please not
mud and screeches all the time.

Why couldn't I be like
the birds in their cages?
And they sent me home.

I didn't mind. A house
with so many birds
is like a tree you've climbed
and can't get down.

Keith Bosley

More wisdom

A wise old owl sat in an oak,
The more he heard the less he spoke;
The less he spoke the more he heard.
Why aren't we all like that wise old bird?

The good and the clever

If all the good people were clever,
And all clever people were good,
The world would be nicer than ever
We thought that it possibly could.

But somehow, 'tis seldom or never
The two hit it off as they should;
The good are so harsh to the clever,
The clever so rude to the good!

Elizabeth Wordsworth

If

If all the seas were one sea,
    What a GREAT sea that would be!
And if all the trees were one tree,
    What a GREAT tree that would be!
And if all the axes were one axe,
    What a GREAT axe that would be!
And if all the men were one man,
    What a GREAT man that would be!
And if the GREAT man took the GREAT axe,
    And cut down the GREAT tree,
And let it fall into the GREAT sea,
    What a splish-splash THAT would be!

Advertising pays . . .

The codfish lays ten thousand eggs,
The homely hen lays one.
The codfish never cackles
To tell you what she's done.
So we scorn the codfish;
While the humble hen we prize.
Which only goes to show—
That it pays to advertise.

. . . sometimes

Beneath this slab
John Brown is stowed.
He watched the ads
And not the road.

Ogden Nash

Wisdom

Tomorrow I'll reform, the fool does say.
Today's too late. The wise did yesterday.

Benjamin Franklin

He who knows

He who knows not, and knows not that he
  knows not, is a fool. Shun him;
He who knows not, and knows that he knows
  not, is a child. Teach him.
He who knows, and knows not that he knows, is
  asleep. Wake him.
He who knows, and knows that he knows, is
  wise. Follow him.

From a Persian proverb

Circles

The white man drew a small circle in the sand
  and told the red man,
  'This is what the Indian knows,'
  and drawing a big circle around the small one,
  'This is what the white man knows.'

The Indian took the stick
  and swept an immense ring around both circles:
  'This is where the white man and the red man
  know nothing.'

Carl Sandburg

Happy thought

The world is so full of a number of things,
I'm sure we should all be as happy as kings.

Robert Louis Stevenson

16
Doing Things

Nothing to do?

Nothing to do?
Nothing to do?
Put some mustard in your shoe,
Fill your pockets full of soot,
Drive a nail into your foot,
Put some sugar in your hair,
Place your toys upon the stair,
Smear some jelly on the latch,
Eat some mud and strike a match,
Draw a picture on the wall,
Roll some marbles down the hall,
Pour some ink in daddy's cap—
   Now go upstairs and take a nap.

Shel Silverstein

Fire pictures

If you lie flat on the hearthrug
   When the fire is all aglow,
And watch just where it's reddest,
   You'll see pictures come and go;
But if you give the tiniest poke
They're sure to vanish into smoke.

Pancakes

Mix a pancake,
Stir a pancake,
   Pop it in the pan;
Fry the pancake,
Toss the pancake—
   Catch it if you can.

Christina Rossetti

Oh, dear, oh!

Oh, dear, oh!
My cake's all dough,
And how to make it better
I do not know.

Paper boat

Make a little paper boat,
Take it to the river;
If it swims and stays afloat,
You will live forever.

Gerda Mayer

Social studies

Woody says, 'Let's *make* our soap.
It's easy.
We learned about it
In school.'
He told Mother,
'All you do is
Take a barrel.
Bore holes in the sides,
And fill it with straw.
Ashes on top—'

'No,' said Mother.

Mary Neville

The useful art of knitting

When Mum sits down to knit at night
Her patterns seem to go just right.
She doesn't even have to look;
She can knit and read a book.
But, oh, the worry
And the flurry
When I sit
And try to knit!
My stitches always get too tight
Or else I drop them out of sight.
I split the wool and big holes come,
I pass my knitting back to Mum.
I grizzle and I grumble,
I struggle and I mumble.
I feel just like that girl Matilda
('The effort very nearly killed her.')
Mum says, 'Don't worry, try once more.'
I throw my knitting on the floor.
We both get cross; I go to bed
And a wonderful dream comes into my head:
When my knitting is finished
I shall win First Prize
for
The Most Original
Best Ventilated
Multi-coloured
Complicated
Scarf
Knitted by a Demented Spider
For an Oddly-shaped Snake
With a Very
Sore Throat.

Katherine Craig

Weather warning

There's no cloud in the sky
    And the swallows fly high
And our faces are suntanned and brown,
    But next week it is camp
And it's sure to be damp;
    The barometer's now going down.
With a long sunny spell
    And a heat-wave as well
It's been almost too hot for a tramp,
    But the glass is at storm
And there's red sky each morn,
    For next week we are going to camp!

Jean Howard

The mudlark

Robert came home from camp today;
He went in the bathtub right away.
There was mud in his hair and round his toes,
Behind his ears and all over his nose.
And you should see his clothes!

'Have you washed yourself while you've been
    away?'
'I went in the river on Wednesday,
And I washed some clothes in the river as well.'
'That would account for their colour and smell.'
'I thought you could tell.'

'There's mud in my 'jamas, and mud in my bed,
And I'm covered with gnat bites right up to my
    head.
My blankets got wet through a hole in the tent,
I cut both my knees, and my penknife's all bent;
My torch has a dent—
But I'm glad that I went.'

It'll take him a week to get himself clean,
So Mummy says, if you know what I mean.
But he's looking so well and feeling so fit,
She doesn't mind Robert and all his kit.
So that's it.

Sylvia Baxendale

Skipping

Little children skip,
The rope so gaily gripping,
    Tom and Harry,
    Jane and Mary,
    Kate, Diana,
    Susan, Anna,
All are fond of skipping!

The grasshoppers all skip,
The early dew-drop sipping,
    Under, over,
    Bent and clover,
    Daisy, sorrel,
    Without quarrel,
All are fond of skipping!

The little boats they skip,
Beside the heavy shipping,
    And while the squalling
    Winds are calling,
    Falling, rising,
    Rising, falling,
All are fond of skipping!

The autumn leaves they skip,
When blasts the trees are stripping;
    Bounding, whirling,
    Sweeping, twirling,
    And in wanton
    Mazes curling,
All are fond of skipping!

Thomas Hood

The ball

Can you catch?
Then watch while I throw it,
Up, ever so high.
White is the ball, so white
On the blue sky.

Run now,
Run under it, quick!
It's beginning to drop—
Drawn by the pull of the ground
To your two hands' cup.

Now you throw it yourself,
Higher yet.
Will it ever come down?
Will it float like a bubble all day
Over paddock and town?

But it hangs
Like a catch in the breath
While the moment expands,
Then faster and faster it speeds
To the cup of my hands.

Lydia Pender

My kite

For my birthday I had a most wonderful kite,
And I took it out quickly to try it in flight.
I went on the moor, where the wind was high;
I held up my kite and begged it to fly.
I saw a bigger boy laughing at me,
'That's not the way, I'll show you,' said he.

He threw up my kite and then let it go,
He pulled the string gently, to and fro.
I could not keep up, for he ran so fast,
But I did not mind, it was flying at last!
Then the wind dropped to a gentle breeze,
And I saw my kite vanish behind the trees.

The boy ran off laughing, he didn't care;
He left the string flying away in the air.
All the way home I cried at my loss;
I could not tell Mother, for fear she'd be cross!
So I ran in the garden to hide away,
And safe, on the path, my lovely kite lay!

Gillian Lowry

The swing

How do you like to go up in a swing,
　Up in the air so blue?
Oh, I do think it the pleasantest thing
　Ever a child can do!

Up in the air and over the wall,
　Till I can see so wide,
Rivers and trees and cattle and all
　Over the countryside—

Till I look down on the garden green,
　Down on the roof so brown—
Up in the air I go flying again,
　Up in the air and down!

Robert Louis Stevenson

Now up, now down

'Shuttlecock, Shuttlecock, up in the air;
Now you are here, now you are there;
Now you can see all the steeples in town;
Now you are up, and now you are down.'

'Shuttlecock, Shuttlecock, with a fine feather,
Isn't it nice to be out in fine weather?
How many times have you been up today?'
'Oh, just as many as down, I should say!'

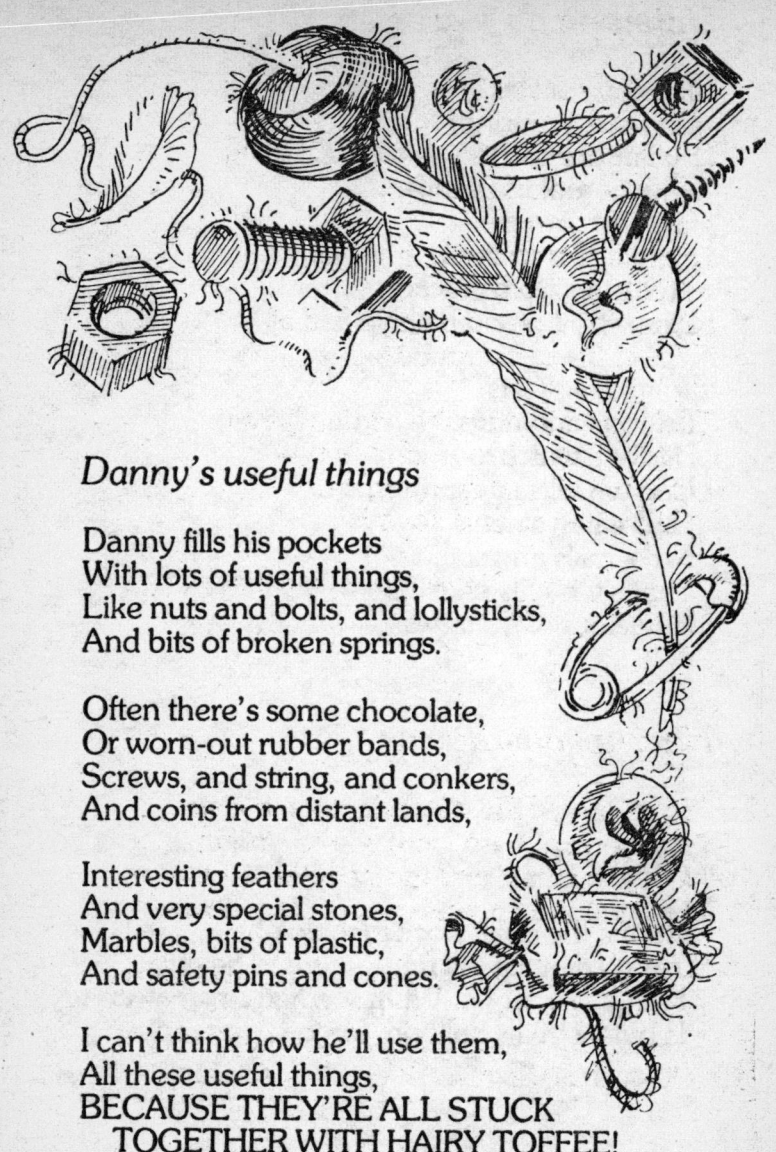

Danny's useful things

Danny fills his pockets
With lots of useful things,
Like nuts and bolts, and lollysticks,
And bits of broken springs.

Often there's some chocolate,
Or worn-out rubber bands,
Screws, and string, and conkers,
And coins from distant lands,

Interesting feathers
And very special stones,
Marbles, bits of plastic,
And safety pins and cones.

I can't think how he'll use them,
All these useful things,
BECAUSE THEY'RE ALL STUCK
    TOGETHER WITH HAIRY TOFFEE!

Sylvia Baxendale

Johnny's pockets

Johnny collects
Conkers on strings,
Sycamore seeds
With aeroplane wings,
Green acorn cups,
Seaweed and shells,
Treasures from crackers
Like whistles and bells.

Johnny collects
Buttons and rings,
Bits of a watch,
Cog wheels and springs,
Half-eaten sweets,
Nuts, nails and screws.
That's why his pockets
Bulge out of his trews.

Alison Winn

Above the dock

Above the quiet dock in midnight,
Tangled in the tall mast's corded height,
Hangs the moon. What seemed so far away
Is but a child's balloon, forgotten after play.

T. E. Hulme

17
Food For Thought

Turtle soup

Beautiful Soup, so rich and green,
Waiting in a hot tureen!
Who for such dainties would not stoop?
Soup of the evening, beautiful Soup!
Soup of the evening, beautiful Soup!
     Beau—ootiful Soo—oop!
     Beau—ootiful Soo—oop!
Soo—oop of the e—e—evening,
     Beautiful, beautiful Soup!

Beautiful Soup! Who cares for fish,
Game, or any other dish?
Who would not give all else for two p
ennyworth only of beautiful soup?
Pennyworth only of beautiful Soup?
     Beau—ootiful Soo—oop!
     Beau—ootiful Soo—oop!
Soo—oop of the e—e—evening,
     Beautiful, beauti—FUL SOUP!

Lewis Carroll

Greedy Jane

'Pudding *and* pie,'
Said Jane; 'Oh my!'
'Which would you rather?'
Said her father.
'Both,' cried Jane,
Quite bold and plain.

A puddin' proverb

'Eat away, chew away, munch and bolt and
    guzzle,
Never leave the table till you're full up to the
    muzzle.'

Norman Lindsay

The sausage

The sausage is a cunning bird
With feathers long and wavy;
It swims about the frying pan
And makes its nest in gravy.

Alas, alack!

Ann, Ann!
  Come! quick as you can!
There's a fish that *talks*
  In the frying-pan.
Out of the fat,
  As clear as glass,
He put up his mouth
  And moaned 'Alas!'
Oh, most mournful,
  'Alas, alack!'
Then turned to his sizzling
  And sank him back.

Walter de la Mare

Eggs and bacon

Eggs and bacon
I like eggs and bacon.
If you think I'm going to sing about it,
You're mistaken.

Traditional Irish children's rhyme

Peas

I eat my peas with honey,
I've done it all my life,
They do taste kind of funny,
But it keeps them on the knife.

Chips

Out of the paper bag
Comes the hot breath of the chips
And I shall blow on them
To stop them burning my lips.

Before I leave the counter
The woman shakes
Raindrops of vinegar on them
And salty snowflakes.

Outside the frosty pavements
Are slippery as a slide
But the chips and I
Are warm inside.

Stanley Cook

Ice-cream

I scream
You scream
We all scream
For ice-cream.

142

18
And So To Bed

New proverb

Early to bed and early to rise
Is the way to feel stupid and have red eyes.

Shirley Brooks

Tumbling

In jumping and tumbling
    We spend the whole day,
Till night by arriving
    Has finished our play.

What then? One and all,
    There's no more to be said,
As we tumbled all day,
    So we tumble to bed.

My bed

Matthew, Mark, Luke and John,
Bless the bed that I lie on.
    Four corners to my bed,
    Four angels round my head;
    One to watch and one to pray
    And two to bear my soul away.

The London bus conductor's prayer

Our Father who art in Hendon,
Holloway be thy name.
Thy Kingston come,
Thy Wimbledon,
In Erith as it is in Epsom.
Give us this Bray our Maidenhead;
And forgive us our bypasses,
As we forgive those who bypass against us.
And lead us not into Thames Ditton..
But deliver us from Esher.
For thine is the Kingston,
The Purley and the Crawley,
For Iver and Iver,
    Crouch End.

Mrs Brown

As soon as I'm in bed at night
And snugly settled down,
The little girl I am by day
Goes very suddenly away,
And then I'm Mrs Brown.

I have a family of six,
And all of them have names,
The girls are Joyce and Nancy Maud,
The boys are Marmaduke and Claude
And Percival and James.

We have a house with twenty rooms
A mile away from town;
I think it's good for girls and boys
To be allowed to make a noise—
And so does Mr Brown.

We do the most exciting things,
Enough to make you creep;
And on and on and on we go—
I sometimes wonder if I know
When I have gone to sleep.

Rose Fyleman

Conversation

'Mother, may I stay up tonight?'
'No, dear.'
'Oh dear! (She always says "No, dear").
But Father said I might.'
'No, dear.'
'He did, that is, if you thought it right.'
'No, dear, it isn't right.'
'Oh dear! Can I keep on the light?'
'No, dear. In spite
Of what your Father said,
You go to bed,
And in the morning you'll be bright
And glad instead
For one more day ahead.'
'I might,
But not for one more night.'
'No, dear – *no*, dear.'
'At least I've been polite, I guess.'
'Yes, dear, you've been polite—
Good night.'
'Oh, dear,
I'd rather stay down here—
I'm quite. . . .'
'No, dear. Now, out of sight.'
'Well that was pretty near—'
'*Good*-night.'
'– all right.'
'Good-*night*!'

David McCord

Index of titles

Index of first lines

Acknowledgements

The authors and publishers would like to thank the following people for giving permission to include in this anthology material which is their copyright. The publishers have made every effort to trace the copyright holders. If we have inadvertently omitted to acknowledge anyone we should be most grateful if this could be brought to our attention for correction at the first opportunity.

George Allen & Unwin Limited for 'Alive without breath' by J. R. R. Tolkien from *The Hobbit*

Angus and Robertson (UK) Limited for 'A house without children' by Keith Bosley from *And I Dance*, and 'A puddin' proverb' by Norman Lindsay from *The Magic Pudding*

Edward Arnold Limited for 'Auntie' and 'Ruthless rhymes' and 'Quiet fun', both by Harry Graham from *More Ruthless Rhymes for Heartless Homes*

Basil Blackwell Publisher for 'Suspension' by Guy Boas from *Domestic Ditties*

William Blackwood & Sons Limited for 'Daddy fell into the pond' by Alfred Noyes

Blyton Books Limited for 'A puzzle poem' by Enid Blyton

Brockhampton Press, now Hodder & Stoughton Children's Books, for 'Johnny's pockets' by Alison Winn from *Helter Skelter*, and 'Out of school' by Hal Summers from *Dawn to Dusk: Poems of Our Time* edited by Charles Causley

Jonathan Cape Limited for 'Grandad' (originally called 'Bucket') and 'Pantomime poem' by Roger McGough from *After the Merrymaking*, and 'Streemin' by Roger McGough from *In the Classroom*

The Ceolfrith Press for 'Paper boat' by Gerda Mayer

William Cole for his poems 'Banananananana' and 'Did you?' and for 'Uncle Umbert' by Shel Silverstein

Charles Connell for 'Counting rhymes' and 'Questions' from *Versicles and Limericks*, published by Beaver Books

Stanley Cook for 'Chips' from *Come Along: Poems for Younger Children* published by the author, 600 Barnsley Road, Sheffield S5 6UA

Curtis Brown Limited, London, on behalf of the Estate of Ogden Nash, for 'Beneath this slab . . .' (originally entitled 'Lather as you go'), 'Family court' and 'Morning prayer'

Piers Davies and Workshop Press Limited for 'The stolen gong song'

Dean & Son Limited for 'My kite' by Gillian Lowry and 'A nursery rhyme puzzle' from *Dean's New Leisure Book for Children*

André Deutsch Limited for 'Fifteen seconds' and 'The Hidebehind' by Michael Rosen from *Mind Your Own Business*, and 'Esau Wood' by Michael Rosen from *Wouldn't You Like to Know*

Dobson Books Limited for 'Rhyme for moles', 'Earth-worm', 'Summer moon' and 'Who?' by Leonard Clark from *Collected Poems and Verses for Children*

Mrs S. L. Dobson for 'Thinking in bed' and 'Come with me' by S. L. Dayman

Mary Mapes Dodge for 'Ten kinds'

Faber & Faber Limited for 'Folks' by Ted Hughes from *Meet My Folks*

Fontana Paperbacks for 'Seal' by William Jay Smith from *The Armada Lion Book of Young Verse* edited by Julia Watson

Martin Gardner for 'Magic word'

Greenwillow Books (A Division of William Morrow & Company) for 'Toucans two' by Jack Prelutsky from *Zoo Doings*

Harcourt, Brace, Jovanovich, Inc, for 'Circles' by Carl Sandburg from *The People, Yes*, 'Arithmetic' from *The Complete Poems of Carl Sandburg*, and 'Questions at night' by Carl Sandburg from *Rainbow in the Sky* edited by Louis Untermeyer

Harper & Row Publishers for 'I woke up this morning' by Karla Kuskin from *The Rose on My Cake*, 'What someone said when he was spanked on the day before his birthday' by John Ciardi from *You Know Who*, and for 'Foolish questions' and 'Oh such silliness!' by William Cole from *Oh, Such Foolishness*

Harrap Limited for 'Conversation', 'LMNTL', 'Scat! Scitten!' and 'Where?' by David McCord from *Mr Bidery's Spidery Garden*

David Higham Associates Limited for 'The milkman' by Clive Sansom from *The Witnesses and Other Poems* published by Methuen & Company Limited, and 'Numbers' and 'School bell' by Eleanor Farjeon from *The Children's Bells* published by Oxford University Press

Hodder & Stoughton Australia for 'Here is the sea' by Jean Chapman from *Velvet Paws and Whiskers*

Richard Lester for 'A cello'

Marian Lines for 'Railway line' from *Tower Blocks: Poems of the City*

Macmillan, London and Basingstoke for 'My dad' from *It's Raining Said John Twaining* by N. M. Bodecker, and 'Late for breakfast' by Mary Dawson from *Allsorts 2*

The Literary Trustees of Walter de la Mare and The Society of Authors as their representative for 'Alas, alack!' by Walter de la Mare from *Collected Poems*

Methuen, London, for 'When I was your age' by Michael Frayn from

Allsorts 7, 'Six' (originally called 'The end') by A. A. Milne from *Now We Are Six*, and 'Mrs Brown' by Rose Fyleman from *The Fairy Green*

Spike Milligan for his poem 'Failure' from *Silly Verse for Kids* published by Puffin Books

Ewart Milne for 'Diamond cut diamond' from *Diamond Cut Diamond* published by The Bodley Head

Oxford University Press for 'W' by James Reeves from *The Blackbird in the Lilac*

Lydia Pender for 'Ruth is six' and 'The ball'

Louis Phillips for 'On nicknames' and 'I always get things right'

Purnell Books for 'Weather warning' by Jean Howard and 'Tied in knots' by Marcia Armitage from *The Girl Guide Annual no. 14*, and 'Jungle calls and Brownie Sue' by Rikki Taylor from *The Brownie Annual 1971*

Michael Rosen and Penguin Books Limited for 'What's your name?', 'Uncle Ted' (originally called 'Going through old photos'), 'Babytalk' (originally called 'When you're a grown-up'), and 'Toothpaste' (originally called 'Who's been at the toothpaste?') from *You Tell Me* by Michael Rosen and Roger McGough

Russell & Volkening, Inc, as agents for the author, for 'Yellow butter' and 'You were the mother last time' by Mary Ann Hoberman

The Scout Association for 'Danny's useful things' by Sylvia Baxendale from *The Cub Scout Annual 1973*, 'The mudlark' by Sylvia Baxendale from *The Cub Scout Annual 1974* and 'Clap your hands' by Colin McKay from *The New Scout Annual 1977*

Jacqueline Segal for 'A blink'

Ian Serraillier for 'I look at you' and 'Cut me, and I'll make you cry' from *I'll Tell You a Tale* published by Penguin Books

The Society of Authors as the literary representative of the Estate of A. E. Housman, and Jonathan Cape Limited, publishers of A. E. Housman, for 'Amelia mixed the mustard' from *Collected Poems of A. E. Housman*

Mrs A. M. Walsh for 'Bus to school' from *The Roundabout by the Sea* by John Walsh

Raymond Wilson for 'Questions' and 'Why?'

William Wise for 'When I grow up' from *Jonathan Blake*

Mrs Arnold C. Woodrich for 'Social studies' by Mary Neville from *Woody and Me*

The World's Work (1913) Limited for 'Who?' by Jane Cattermull from *Elizabethan Poetry Award Competition* © 1967

The Writer's Literary Agency, Florida, and Robert D. Hoeft for 'If things grew down' by Robert D. Hoeft

More Beaver Books

We hope you have enjoyed this book. Here are some of the other poetry collections published by Beaver Books:

The Beaver Book of Creepy Verse A Beaver original. A fascinating collection full of ghosts, ghouls, witches, monsters, ogres, spells and curses – some terrifying, some funny – and all guaranteed to send a shiver down your spine. Chosen by Zenka and Ian Woodward and chillingly illustrated by William Geldart

The Beaver Book of Animal Verse A Beaver original. A beautiful collection of poetry about all kinds of animals, compiled by Raymond Wilson, with superb line drawings by Tessa Barwick

The Beaver Book of Skool Verse A Beaver original. An amazing collection of poems and verses about school, including playground rhymes and games, mnemonics, verses about school dinners, lessons, teachers, end of term and exams. Lots of the material came from children all over the country who sent in their favourite rhymes, and the collection was put together by Jennifer Curry, with cartoons by Graham Thompson

These and many other Beavers are available from your local bookshop or newsagent, or can be ordered direct from: Hamlyn Paperback Cash Sales, PO Box 11, Falmouth, Cornwall TR10 9EN. Send a cheque or postal order made payable to the Hamlyn Publishing Group, for the price of the book plus postage at the following rates:
UK: 45p for the first book, 20p for the second book, and 14p for each additional book ordered to a maximum charge of £1.63;
BFPO and Eire: 45p for the first book, 20p for the second book, plus 14p per copy for the next 7 books and thereafter 8p per book;
OVERSEAS: 75p for the first book and 21p for each extra book.

New Beavers are published every month and if you would like the *Beaver Bulletin*, a newsletter which tells you about new books and gives a complete list of titles and prices, send a large stamped addressed envelope to:

Beaver Bulletin
The Hamlyn Group
Astronaut House
Feltham
Middlesex TW14 9AR

206106